The Ultimately Hilarious

Joke Book

First paperback edition July 2022

Book design by Jessica McNamara

ISBN 979-8-8398-3754-6 (paperback)

Williams Heart Publishing
www.williamsheartpublishing.com

Contents

Contents
continued...

About this Book

When I was a kid I loved jokes. In fact, I loved jokes so much that once I made my brother wet his pants with laughter. I was sure that when I grew up I would be a comedian, and I practiced telling jokes all day every day.

But as I got older, I started to think about other things I wanted to do instead of being a joker. When I was fifteen I began training to set a world record for weightlifting on the moon. I worked really hard at this for a couple of years until I realized I obviously can't go to the moon because I am allergic to cheese (and rumor has it the moon is made of cheese).

After my moon weightlifting dream ended, I decided to become a unicorn helmet engineer. I felt bad that unicorns didn't have any protection for their horns and I wanted to help them with this. I made some really great prototypes but despite searching every forest on earth I couldn't find any unicorns to test my helmet.

Just as I was about to start my new career as a snowman hunter in the Sahara Desert, my son was born. He loved jokes too and I was so happy to share my love of laughter with him. But then, my son started actually TELLING jokes.

Well, between you and me, I have a secret to tell you. His jokes were NOT funny. Like, not at all. He tried and tried but every new joke he told was even less funny than the last one. He would tell jokes like:
- What is something that is funny? A joke.
- Why did Superman go to the supermarket? to buy groceries!
Do you see what I mean? So after a few years of listening to these terrible jokes, I decided to help him out once and for all and came up with a plan to collect some of the funniest jokes I could find and I ended up collecting over 1000 hilarious jokes. Now I've put them all together in this easy to read book so I can share them with the world!

Jokes have been around since the beginning of time. In fact, most jokes have been around for so long that it's impossible to trace them back to their original creators. I collected all of the jokes for this book from various places and although I tried very hard, I was unable to find out who actually wrote these jokes to start off with. In a way, jokes belong to everyone, but it is important to remember that every joke started out as somebody else's funny idea and if you ever find that person, remember to say thank you.

Happy Joking!

Animal Jokes

> What do you get when you cross a Labrador and a magician?
>
> -A Larbacadabrador

HA HA HA

How do you say goodbye to a poodle?
- Poodle-oo

What did the dog say when he sat on sandpaper?
- Ruff!

What did the horse say when it fell?
- I've fallen and I can't giddyup!

What did the teacher say when the horse walked into the class?
-Why the long face?

What do you call a cat wearing shoes?
- Puss in Boots

What kind of sports cars do cats drive?
- Fur-arris

What do you call a cow with no legs?
- Ground Beef

What do you call a sleeping bull?
- A Bull-Dozer

Why do gorillas have big nostrils?
- Because they have big fingers!

Why do fish live in saltwater?
- Because pepper makes them sneeze

How does a lion greet other lions?
- Pleased to eat you

What did the judge say when the skunk walked into the courtroom?
- Odor in the court!

What do you call an alligator who solves mysteries?
-An Investigator

Can a wallaby jump higher than a building?
- Of course, buildings can't jump!

What do you call a cow spying on another cow?
- A steak out

What goes "Ooo Ooo Ooo"?
- A cow with no lips

What do you call a thieving alligator?
- A crook-o-dile

Why did the fish blush?
- It saw the ocean's bottom

Why do pandas like old movies?
- Because they play in black and white

What's black and white and red all over?
-A sunburned zebra

Who stole the soap out of the bathtub?
- The robber ducky

What time does a duck wake up?
- The quack of dawn

What dog keeps the best time?
- A watchdog

What kind of snake would you find on a car?
- A windshield Viper

What kind of facial hair does a moose have?
- A moostache

What do you call a dead fly?
- A flew

What do you call a sleeping dinosaur?
- A Dino-Snore

What did the duck say when he bought lipstick?
- Put it on my bill

How do you count cows?
- With a cowculator

Where do mice park their boats?
- At the hickory dickory dock

What do you call two octopuses that look exactly the same?
- Itenticle

Where do you find a dog with no legs?
- Right where you left it

Why is a bee's hair always sticky?
- Because it uses a honey comb

What do you call a dinosaur that never gives up?
- A try and try and try-ceratops

Why does a giraffe have such a long neck?
- Because his feet stink

What do you call an exploding monkey?
- A baboom

What do you call a cow that eats grass?
-A lawn moo-er

What do cats have for breakfast?
- Mice krispies

Why can't dinosaurs clap?
- Because they're dead

What do a shark and a computer have in common?
- They both have mega-bytes

What are caterpillars afraid of?
- Dogger-pillars

What do you call a penguin in the desert?
- Lost

What do you call a lazy baby kangaroo?
- A pouch potato

Why did the pig have ink all over its face?
- Because it came out of the pen

Why do dogs float in water?
- Because they are good buoys

What do you call an elephant that doesn't matter?
- An irrelephant

What do you call a deer with no eyes?
- No idea!

What do you call a fish wearing a bowtie?
- Sofishticated

How does a penguin build its house?
- Igloos it together

Birthday Jokes

What did the pirate say on his 80th birthday?
- Aye Matey

What do you say to a kangaroo on its birthday?
- Hoppy birthday

What sort of birthday cake do ghosts prefer?
- I scream cake

What goes up and never comes down?
- Your Age

Why do we put candles on top of birthday cakes?
- Because it's too hard to put them on the bottom

What do you always get on your birthday?
- Another year older

What does a witch do on her birthday?
- She Spellebrates

Where do you buy a birthday present for a cat?
- From a cat-alogue

Why couldn't the knot go to the birthday party?
- It was all tied up

What kind of candle burns longer than others?
- None, they all burn shorter!

Where can you go to study birthday treats?
- Sundae School

What does an oyster do on its birthday?
- Shellebrates

What kind of music do balloons fear?
- Pop music

Why did the birthday cake go to the doctor's?
- Because it was feeling crumby

Why does the mushroom always get invited to birthday parties?
- He's a fun guy (fungi)

What does every birthday end with?
- The letter Y

What birthday present is guaranteed
to make anyone's face light up?
- A light bulb

What did the ocean say on its birthday?
- Nothing - it just waved

What song do you sing at a snowman's
birthday party?
- Freeze a jolly good fellow

What do you call a noodle
pretending it's his birthday?
- An impasata

What kind of jewelry did the rabbit
wear for its birthday?
- 14 carrot gold

What's worse than finding a bug in
your birthday cake?
- Finding half a bug

What's the difference between a pie and a birthday cake?
- Pie are squared, cakes are round

What did the frog drink to wash down his birthday cake?
- Diet croak

What games do rabbits play at their birthday parties?
- Musical hares

Why did the little girl get soap for her birthday?
- It was a soap-rise party

Why were there balloons in the bathroom?
- There was a birthday potty

What does a cat dance to at parties?
- Mewsic

What do computers want for their birthdays?
- An upgrade

Joke Writing Tip:

NEVER BE MEAN

SOMETIMES WHEN WE ARE WRITING OR TELLING JOKES IT MIGHT SEEM FUNNY TO BE MEAN OR MAKE A MEAN JOKE ABOUT SOMEONE ELSE. SOMETIMES, PEOPLE MIGHT EVEN LAUGH AT THESE JOKES. BUT THE TRUTH IS, MEAN JOKES DON'T REALLY MAKE PEOPLE HAPPY, AND THEY DEFINITELY DON'T MAKE THE PERSON WHO YOU ARE BEING MEAN TO HAPPY. THE WHOLE POINT OF JOKES IS TO BRING HAPPINESS TO THE PEOPLE AROUND YOU. SO REMEMBER, ALWAYS THINK ABOUT OTHERS WHEN YOU WRITE YOUR JOKES, AND MAKE SURE THAT NOBODY IS GOING TO GET UPSET OR OFFENDED WHEN YOU TELL YOUR JOKE AND THEN YOU ARE GOOD TO GO!

Corny Jokes

What did the policeman say to his belly button?
- You're under a vest

What do you call a pig that does karate?
- A pork chop

Why shouldn't you write with a broken pencil?
- It's pointless

Why did the bike fall over?
- It was two tired

Why did the scarecrow win an award?
- He was outstanding in his field

Why did the golfer wear two pairs of pants?
- In case he got a hole in one

Where do pirates get their hooks?
- The second-hand store

What kind of ghost has the best hearing?
- The eeriest

What do you call a factory that makes okay products?
- A satis-factory

What does a baby computer call its father?
- Data

Why are there gates around cemeteries?
- Because people are dying to get in

What's brown and sticky?
- A stick

How do you make an octopus laugh?
- With ten-tickles

What do you get when you cross a lemon and a cat?
- A sour-puss

Why do seagulls fly over the sea?
- If they flew over the bay, they would be bagels

What do you call birds that stick together?
- Vel-crows

If athletes get athletes' foot, what do elves get?
- Mistle-toe

What do you call a snake wearing a hard hat?
-A boa constructor

Why did the baby strawberry cry?
- His parents were in a jam

What did the right eye say to the left eye?
- Between you and me, something smells

How do you tell if a vampire is sick?
- See if he is coffin

What happens when frogs park illegally?
- They got toad

Why do you never see elephants hiding in trees?
- Because they are really good at it

What do you call a fish without eyes?
- Fsh

What did the tomato say to the other tomato during a race?
- Bet you can't ketchup

Why did the photograph go to jail?
- Because it was framed

Why do pancakes always win at baseball?
- They have the best batter

What has four wheels and flies?
- A garbage truck

Why should you always knock on a refrigerator door before opening it?
- In case there's a salad dressing

What do you call a bear with no teeth?
- A gummy bear

Why can't you hear a pterodactyl going to the bathroom?
- Because the P is silent

What kind of music do mummies listen to?
- Wrap music

What do lawyers wear to work?
- Lawsuits

Bacon and eggs walk into a cafe, the waitress said
"Sorry, we don't serve breakfast"

Why should you never use "beef stew" as a password?
- Because it's not stroganoff

Why is the grass so dangerous?
- It's full of blades

How did the barber win the race?
- He knew a shortcut

What kind of cheese isn't yours?
- Nacho cheese

How do you turn soup into jewelry?
- Add 24 carrots

Why are spiders so smart?
- They can find everything on the web

Spring is here! I got so excited
I wet my plants!

What do you call a shoe made from
a banana?
- A slipper

What's orange and sounds like a
parrot?
- A carrot

What do you call a blind dinosaur?
- A do-you-think-he-saw-us

What did the janitor say when he jumped out of the closet?
- Supplies!

What did one hat say to the other hat?
- You stay here. I'll go on ahead

Why did the stadium get hot after the game?
- All of the fans left

Why was the broom late for work?
- It over-swept

What do you call someone with no body and no nose?
- Nobody Knows

How does the moon cut his hair?
- Eclipse it

Dad Jokes

Sundays are always a little sad, but the day before is a sadder day

RIP boiling water,
you will be mist

Mountains aren't just funny, they're
hill areas

Hey, is your butt broken?
Because I can see a giant crack down
the middle

I once wrote a song about a tortilla,
but it's more of a wrap

I'm reading a book about anti-gravity,
it's impossible to put down

Did you hear about the kidnapping
at school?
It's okay, he woke up

I started a band called 999 megabytes,
we still haven't gotten a gig

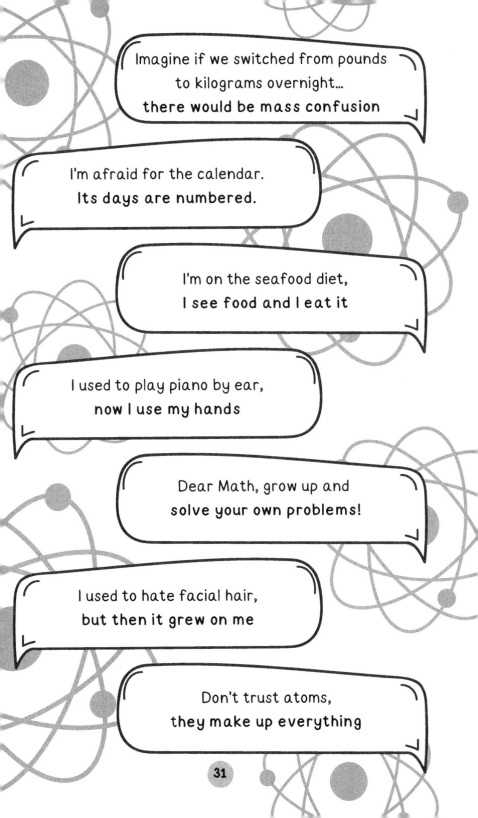

Imagine if we switched from pounds
to kilograms overnight...
there would be mass confusion

I'm afraid for the calendar.
Its days are numbered.

I'm on the seafood diet,
I see food and I eat it

I used to play piano by ear,
now I use my hands

Dear Math, grow up and
solve your own problems!

I used to hate facial hair,
but then it grew on me

Don't trust atoms,
they make up everything

31

I ordered a chicken and an egg online,
I'll let you know

I only know 25 letters of the alphabet.
I don't know Y.

Dad, can you put the cat out?
I didn't know it was on fire!

Are you alright?
No, I'm half left

Did you hear about the restaurant on the moon?
It had no atmosphere

Wanna hear a joke about paper?
Never mind - it's tearable

I'd tell you a joke about construction,
but I'm still working on it

My boss told me to have a good day,
so I went home

I know a lot of jokes about retired people,
but none of them work

I don't trust trees,
they seem kinda shady

Singing in the shower is fun until you get soap in your mouth,
then it becomes a soap opera

Dogs can't operate MRI machines,
but catscan

I don't trust stairs,
they're always up to something

I was going to tell a time-traveling joke,
but you guys didn't like it

Sore throats are a
pain in the neck

Dad, did you get a haircut?
No, I got them all cut

You know, some people say they
pick their nose, but I feel like I was
just born with mine

I like telling dad jokes...
sometimes he laughs

I got hit in the head with a can of
Coke today. Don't worry, I'm not hurt,
it was a soft drink.

Do you wanna box for your leftovers?
No, but I'll wrestle you for them

What kind of car does an egg drive?
A yolkswagon

What do you call it when a snowman throws a tantrum?
A meltdown.

Can February March?
No, but April May

If a child refuses a nap, are they guilty of
resisting a rest?

What is the best time to go to the dentist?
Tooth-hurty

A cheese factory exploded in France.
Da brie is everywhere!

I'm so good at sleeping,
I can do it with my eyes closed!

I slept like a log last night,
I woke up in the fireplace

Four-thirds of people admit that they're **bad with fractions**

Someone glued my pack of cards together, **I don't know how to deal with it**

I was wondering why the frisbee kept looking bigger and bigger, **and then it hit me**

I have a fear of speed bumps, **I'm slowly getting over it**

I can kayak, **canoe?**

I made a pencil with two erasers, **it was pointless**

(Say this when the car is reversing) **"Ahhh - this takes me back"**

Doctor Jokes

How do you get a sick pig to the hospital?
In an hambulance!

When does a doctor get mad?
- When he runs out of patients

What did the doctor say to the rocket ship?
- Time to get your booster shot

Why did the pillow go to the doctor?
- He was feeling stuffed up

What do you do if you hurt your foot while driving?
- Call a toe-truck

If an apple a day keeps the doctor away, what does an onion do?
- Keeps everyone away

Why did the paintbrush see a doctor?
- It had a stroke

What's the worst thing about seasickness?
- It comes in waves

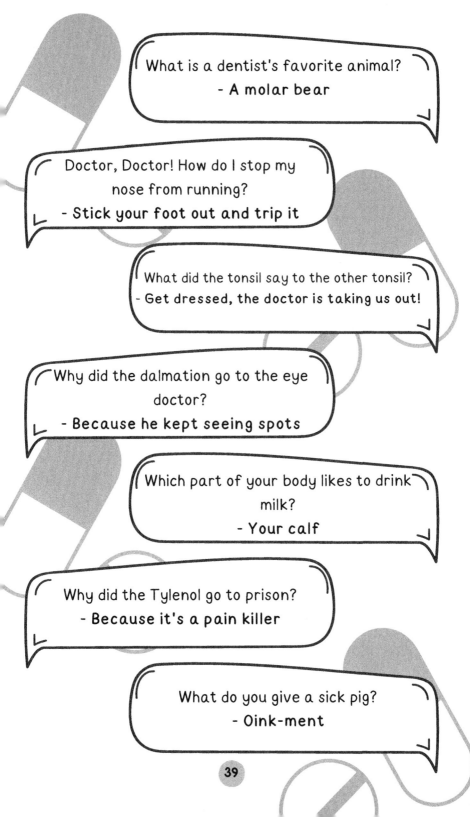

What is a dentist's favorite animal?
- A molar bear

Doctor, Doctor! How do I stop my nose from running?
- Stick your foot out and trip it

What did the tonsil say to the other tonsil?
- Get dressed, the doctor is taking us out!

Why did the dalmation go to the eye doctor?
- Because he kept seeing spots

Which part of your body likes to drink milk?
- Your calf

Why did the Tylenol go to prison?
- Because it's a pain killer

What do you give a sick pig?
- Oink-ment

39

Where do horses go when they're sick?
- The Horsepital

How did the centipede run up a million-dollar doctor bill?
- He sprained his ankle

Did you hear the one about the germ?
- Never mind, I don't want to spread it around

What does a dentist call her x-rays?
- Tooth-pics

Why do nurses bring red markers to work?
- Just in case they need to draw blood

Why did the cookie go to the hospital?
- He was feeling really crumby

Why did the tree go to the dentist?
- To get a root canal

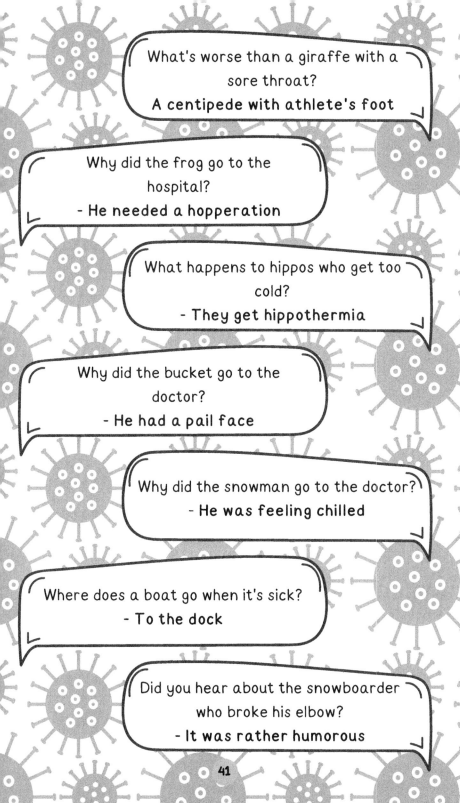

What's worse than a giraffe with a sore throat?
A centipede with athlete's foot

Why did the frog go to the hospital?
- He needed a hopperation

What happens to hippos who get too cold?
- They get hippothermia

Why did the bucket go to the doctor?
- He had a pail face

Why did the snowman go to the doctor?
- He was feeling chilled

Where does a boat go when it's sick?
- To the dock

Did you hear about the snowboarder who broke his elbow?
- It was rather humorous

41

Where did the duck go when he felt sick?
- To the duck-tor

Why did the balloon go to the doctor?
- It was feeling light-headed

What do you give a sick bird?
- Tweet-ment

Why did the computer go to the doctor?
- It had a virus

Why did the witch go to the doctor?
- She had a dizzy spell

What's the most common operation in a toy hospital?
- Plastic Surgery

What smells the best at dinner?
- Your nose

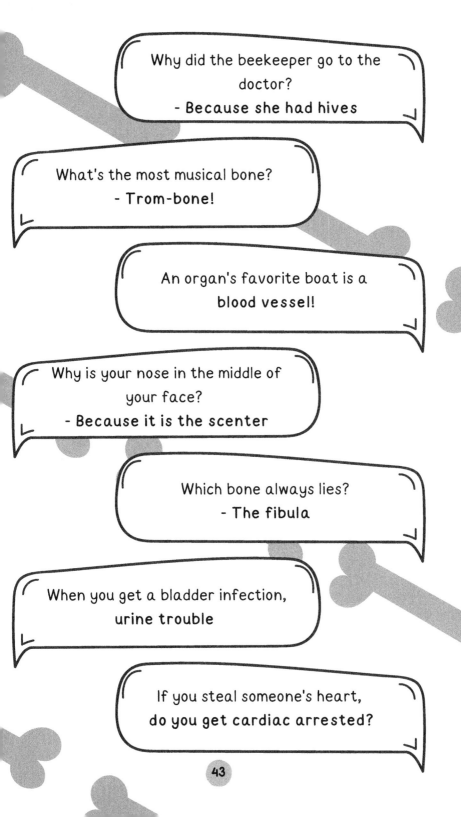

Why did the beekeeper go to the doctor?
- Because she had hives

What's the most musical bone?
- Trom-bone!

An organ's favorite boat is a blood vessel!

Why is your nose in the middle of your face?
- Because it is the scenter

Which bone always lies?
- The fibula

When you get a bladder infection, urine trouble

If you steal someone's heart, do you get cardiac arrested?

43

Why did the brain go for a run?
- **To jog its memory**

The brain is an amazing organ,
it really makes you think

Why did the surgeon put makeup on
his brain?
- **To make up his mind**

Did you hear about the guy who lost
his whole left side?
- **He's all right now**

Doctor: You are very sick.
Patient: Can I get a second opinion?
Doctor: Yes, of course, you are very ugly
too!

Patient: Doctor, I keep hearing a
ringing sound.
Doctor: Answer the phone

Patient: Doctor, sometimes I feel
like I'm invisible.
Doctor: Who said that

Food Jokes

What did the frog order at the burger place?
- French flies and a diet croak

HA HA HA

HA HA HA

What's the best way to burn vegetables?
- Roast them

What did the baby corn say to its mom?
- Where is pop corn?

How do you know carrots are good for your eyes?
- Have you ever seen a rabbit wearing glasses?

What is black, white, green, and bumpy?
- A pickle wearing a tuxedo

When potatoes have babies, what are they called?
- Tater tots

How fast is milk?
- It's pasteurized before you know it

Why did the melon jump into the lake?
- It wanted to be a watermelon

Why did the skeleton go to the barbecue?
- **To get another rib**

What is a table you can eat?
- **A vegetable**

What is the best thing to put into a pie?
- **Your teeth!**

Why did the banana go to the doctor?
- **Because it wasn't peeling well**

What do you call a peanut in a spacesuit?
- **An astronut**

What can't you eat at dinner?
- **Breakfast and lunch**

Wanna hear a joke about pizza?
- **Never mind, it's too cheesy**

Why shouldn't you tell an egg a joke?
- Because it might crack up

Which friends should you take out to dinner?
- Your taste buds

What day do potatoes hate most?
- Fry-day

What do bananas do when they get a sunburn?
- They peel

Waiter, will my pizza be long?
- No sir, it will be round

What did the plate whisper to the other plate?
- Dinner is on me

What is an elephant's favorite vegetable?
- Squash

Which vegetable has just broken out of prison?
- An escapea

What's the most relaxing type of pasta?
- Spa-ghetti

Did you hear the joke about the peanut butter?
I'm not telling you, you might spread it!

What kind of nuts always seem to have a cold?
- Cashews

What did the taco say to the burrito?
- Where you bean?

What do elves make sandwiches with?
- Shortbread

What is an astronaut's favorite food?
- Launch meat

What do cats call mice on skateboards?
- Meals on Wheels

Where do tough chickens come from?
- Hard-boiled eggs

What's a pretzel's favorite dance?
- The twist

How do you measure the weight of crackers?
- In grahams

What do you give a sick lemon?
- Lemon-aid

What two candies are the smartest?
- Smarties and nerds

What are sailors' enemies?
- Leeks

What do you get when you put three ducks in a box?
- A box of quackers

What did the cake say to the fork?
- "You want a piece of me?"

What do you get if you cross a cow with a smurf?
- Blue cheese

Why couldn't the hamburger stop making jokes?
- He was on a roll!

Why did the student eat her exam?
- The teacher told her it was a piece of cake

What do you call a cranky pea?
- Grum-pea

What fish do you eat with peanut butter?
- A jellyfish

Why does the yogurt love going to the museum?
- Because it's cultured

What has ears but can't hear?
- A cornfield

What's brown, hairy, and wears sunglasses?
- A coconut on vacation

What does garlic do when it gets hot?
- It takes its cloves off

What does a lemon say when it answers the phone?
- Yellow!

What do you call a hotdog on wheels?
- Fast food

What is a cat's favorite dessert?
- Chocolate Mouse

Gross Jokes

What comes out of your
nose at 150 mph?
- Lamborgreeny

What do you call it when someone has a ton of gas after eating?
- A fart attack

What did the booger say to the finger?
- Pick on someone your own size

Where does your nose go when it gets hungry?
- Booger king

What happened to the man who only ate skittles?
- He farted rainbows

What do you find inside a clean nose?
- Fingerprints

What's the smelliest city in America?
- Phew York

Why couldn't the skeleton fart in front of his friends?
- He didn't have the guts

What do you call a fart from a butt that's fallen asleep?
- A snore

What's the difference between a plate and a booger?
- The plate is on the table, but the booger is under it

What's the difference between broccoli and boogers?
- Kids don't eat broccoli

What monster fits on the end of your finger?
- The bogeyman

What time do butts get up?
- At the crack of dawn

What do you do if you find a bear on your toilet?
- Let it finish

Did you hear about the dinosaur that farted?
- It was a blast from the past

What do you call someone who refuses to fart in public?
- A private tutor

What did one nostril say to the other nostril?
- You think you're better than me, but you're snot

What color is a burp?
- Burple

Why did the zombie take a sick day?
- He was feeling really rotten

Why did the butt band fail?
- Their music sounded like crap

What do you see when a duck pulls down his underwear?
- His butt quack

Why did the priest need new underwear?
- Because they were so holy

What do you call it when you are startled by a fart?
- Fartled

What's gooey, yellow, and smells like bananas?
- Monkey snot

What happened to the blind skunk?
- He fell in love with a fart

Why did the woman stop telling fart jokes?
- Everyone told her they stink

Why do ducks have feathers?
- To cover their butt-quack

How do you make a regular bath into a bubble bath?
- Eat beans for dinner

What's the definition of a surprise?
- A fart with a lump in it

Joke Writing Tip:

Know Your Audience

A joke is only funny if the person you are telling it to thinks it is funny. This means that you have to think about who is hearing your joke and what sort of things they might find funny before you start joking. Some things you might want to think about are the age, gender, hobbies and interests of the person you are talking to. Think about how well you know this person, and what sort of things usually make them laugh. For example, a little kid will probably laugh if you tell them a joke about poo, but a grandma might not be so impressed by toiler humor. Remember, just because you think it is funny does not mean your audience will!

Holiday Jokes

Where did the sheep go on vacation?

- The Baaahamas

What are baby witches called?
- Halloweenies

How does the Easter Bunny keep his fur looking so nice?
- He uses hare spray

What happens if you eat Christmas decorations?
- You get tinselitus

What is the Easter Bunny's favorite kind of music?
- Hip Hop

Why didn't the coffee bean go to the Halloween party?
- Because it was grounded

What happens when you wear a watch on a plane?
- Time flies

Where do bees go on their holiday?
- Stingapore

What did the pig say on a hot summer day?
- I'm bacon

Where do cows go on vacation?
- Moo York

What do you call Santa when he stops moving?
- Santa Pause

Why didn't the elephant carry a suitcase?
- He already had a trunk

Where does Christmas come before Easter?
- The dictionary

What does a farmer grow on January 1st?
- New Year's Hay

What did the fisherman say on Halloween?
- Trick or trout

What is a cow's favorite holiday?
- Moo years day

Why wouldn't the Christmas tree stand up?
- Because it had no legs

What did the dad say at 11:59 on New Year's Eve?
- I promise not to make any bad jokes for the rest of the year

What do you get when you cross a snake and a plane?
- A Boeing Constrictor

How do you find out the weather when you're on vacation?
- Go outside and look up

How do you fix a broken jack-o-lantern?
- With a pumpkin patch

Where do ghosts go on vacation?
- The Boohamas

What do you get when you pour hot water into a rabbit hole?
- Hot cross bunnies

How does a sheep say merry Christmas?
- Fleece Navidad

What wears a red suit and goes "oh, oh, oh"?
- Santa walking backward

What do you get when you cross a rabbit with a shellfish?
- An oyster bunny

What did the bird say on Halloween?
- Twick or Tweet

Where do ghosts like to go on vacation?
- Lake Eerie

Why do mummies like Christmas so much?
- Because of all the wrapping

What do farmers give their wives on New Year's Eve
- Hogs and Kisses

What happened to the Easter Bunny when he misbehaved at school?
- He was eggspelled

Who delivers Christmas presents to elephants?
- Elephanta Clause

What is corns favorite day?
- New ears day

What travels around the world but stays in one place?
- A stamp

What do snowmen like most about school?
- Snow and tell

What is a cow's favorite night of the year?
- Moo Year's Eve

Why do birds fly south for New Year's Eve?
- Too far to walk

I'll never travel to Finland, I'm afraid I'll disappear into...
FinnAir

How does the Easter Bunny stay fit?
- Eggs-ercise

Where did the pencil go for summer vacation?
- Pencil-vania

What do dogs say on New Year's Eve?
- Woof

What do you call a snowman in summer?
- A puddle

What's the easiest way to keep your New Year's resolution to read more?
- Put subtitles on the TV

What does Steven like to be called
on New Year's Eve?
- **New Year's Steve**

What is a Christmas tree's favorite
candy?
- **Orna-mints**

Where do hamsters like to go on
vacation?
- **Hamsterdam**

Where does pepperoni go on
vacation?
- **The leaning tower of Pizza**

What does an elf study in school?
- **The elfabet**

Why did the bear cross the road?
- **Because the chicken was on
vacation**

Where do sharks go on their
holiday?
- **Finland**

Knock Knock Jokes

Knock Knock
Who's there?
Smell mop
Smell mop who?
No, I won't smell your poo!

Knock Knock
Who's there?
Anita
Anita who?
Let me in, Anita borrow something

Knock Knock
Who's there?
Leaf
Leaf who?
Leaf me alone!

Knock Knock
Who's there?
Nana
Nana who?
Nana your business!

Knock Knock
Who's there?
I am
I am who?
You don't know who you are?

Knock Knock
Who's there?
Butter
Butter who?
I butter not tell you

Knock Knock
Who's there?
Broccoli
Broccoli who?
Um, Broccoli doesn't have a last name silly!

68

Knock Knock
Who's there?
Roach
Anita who?
I roach you a letter, still waiting for a reply

Knock Knock
Who's there?
Amish
Amish who?
You're a shoe? Uh, okay

Knock Knock
Who's there?
Tank
Tank who?
You're Welcome

Knock Knock
Who's there?
Nuisance
Nuisance who?
What's new since yesterday?

Knock Knock
Who's there?
Taco
Taco who?
Taco to you later, this is taking too long

Knock Knock
Who's there?
Alpaca
Alpaca who?
Alpaca the suitcase, you load the car

Knock Knock
Who's there?
Barbara
Barbara who?
Barbara black sheep
have you any wool

Knock Knock
Who's there?
Luke
Luke who?
Luke through the
peephole and see

Knock Knock
Who's there?
Goliath
Goliath who?
Goliath down, you
look-eth tired

Knock Knock
Who's there?
Mustache
Mustache who?
I mustache you a
question but i'll shave it
for later

Knock Knock
Who's there?
A herd
A herd who?
A herd you were home so
I came over

Knock Knock
Who's there?
Nobel
Nobel who?
No bell, that's why I
knocked

Knock Knock
Who's there?
Doris
Doris who?
Doris locked, that's why
I'm knocking

Knock Knock
Who's there?
Canoe
Canoe who?
Canoe come out now?

Knock Knock
Who's there?
Europe
Europe who?
Europe early this
morning

Knock Knock
Who's there?
Spell
Spell who?
W.H.O

Knock Knock
Who's there?
Kanga
Kanga who?
Actually, it's kangaroo

Knock Knock
Who's there?
Dishes
Dishes who?
Dish is a nice place!

71

Knock Knock
Who's there?
Figs
Figs who?
Figs the doorbell, it's not working

Knock Knock
Who's there?
Theodore
Theodore who?
Theodore wasn't open so I knocked

Knock Knock
Who's there?
Wooden shoe
Wooden shoe who?
Wooden shoe like to hear another joke

Knock Knock
Who's there?
Orange
Orange who?
Orange you going to let me in?

Knock Knock
Who's there?
Viper
Viper who?
Viper nose, it's running!

Knock Knock
Who's there?
Ash
Ash who?
Bless you

Knock Knock
Who's there?
Will
Will who?
Will you just open the door already!

Knock Knock
Who's there?
Ida
Ida who?
Ida know, I forgot

Knock Knock
Who's there?
Interrupting cow
Interrupting co....
MOOOOOO!!!!!

Knock Knock
Who's there?
Cook
Cook who?
Yes you are

Knock Knock
Who's there?
Olive
Olive who?
Olive you too

Knock Knock
Who's there?
Wendy
Wendy who?
Wendy bell works, I won't have to knock

Knock Knock
Who's there?
Europe
Europe who?
No I'm not!

Knock Knock
Who's there?
FBI
FB....
We are asking the
questions here!

Knock Knock
Who's there?
Bamb
Bamb who?
Bamboo is what pandas
eat, let's have pizza

Knock Knock
Who's there?
Little old lady
Little old lady who?
Hey, you can yodel!

Knock Knock
Who's there?
Frank
Frank who?
Frank you for being my
friend

Knock Knock
Who's there?
Interrupting pirate
Interrupting pira...
ARGHHHHHHH!!!!!

Knock Knock
Who's there?
Alex
Alex who?
Alex-plain when you open the door

Knock Knock
Who's there?
Cook
Cook who?
What, are you a clock now?

Knock Knock
Who's there?
Robin
Robin who?
Robin you, now hand over the cash!

Knock Knock
Who's there?
Needle
Needle who?
Needle little money, please let me in

Knock Knock
Who's there?
Justin
Justin who?
Justin the neighborhood so came over

Knock Knock
Who's there?
Who
Who who?
I didn't know you were an owl

Knock Knock
Who's there?
Tennis
Tennis who?
Tennis five plus five

Knock Knock
Who's there?
Nun
Nun who?
Nun-ya business

Knock Knock
Who's there?
Horsp
Horsp who?
Did you just say horse poo?

Knock Knock
Who's there?
No one
No one who?
....
(Remain silent)

Knock Knock
Who's there?
Cargo
Cargo who?
No, cargo "beep beep"

Knock Knock
Who's there?
Arfur
Arfur who?
Arfur-got

Knock Knock
Who's there?
Ida
Ida who?
It's pronounced Idaho

Knock Knock
Who's there?
Howard
Howard who?
Howard I know?

Knock Knock
Who's there?
I did up
I did up who?
You did a poo?

Knock Knock
Who's there?
Amanda
Amanda who?
Amanda fix your door

Knock Knock
Who's there?
Witches
Witches who?
Witches the way home?

Knock Knock
Who's there?
Anita puh
Anita puh who?
Eww, find a toilet!

79

Knock Knock
Who's there?
Althea
Althea who?
Althea later, alligator

Knock Knock
Who's there?
Harry
Harry who?
Harry up, it's cold!

Knock Knock
Who's there?
Norma Lee
Norma Lee who?
Norma Lee I don't knock
on strange doors

Knock Knock
Who's there?
Ice cream soda
Ice cream soda who?
Ice cream so da people
can hear me

Knock Knock
Who's there?
Deja
Deja who?
Knock Knock

Knock Knock
Who's there?
Carrot
Carrot who?
Carrot-e-chop
HYAH

Knock Knock
Who's there?
Lettuce
Lettuce who?
Lettuce in

Knock Knock
Who's there?
Alien
Alien who?
Uh, how many aliens do
you know?

Knock Knock
Who's there?
Sweden
Sweden who?
Sweden sour chicken

Knock Knock
Who's there?
Annie
Annie who?
Annie body home?

Knock Knock
Who's there?
Adore
Adore who?
Adore is between us so
open up

Knock Knock
Who's there?
Poop
Poop who?
Haha, you said poo
twice

Knock Knock
Who's there?
Annie
Annie who?
Annie thing you can do, I can do better

Knock Knock
Who's there?
Mikey
Mikey who?
Mikey doesn't fit in the keyhole

Knock Knock
Who's there?
Double
Double who?
W

Knock Knock
Who's there?
Ya
Ya who?
I'm excited to see you too

Knock Knock
Who's there?
Pecan
Pecan who?
Pecan someone your own size

Knock Knock
Who's there?
Wire
Wire who?
Wire you always asking who's there?

Knock Knock
Who's there?
Candice
Candice who?
Candice joke get any worse?

Knock Knock
Who's there?
Amos
Amos who?
Amos-quito

Knock Knock
Who's there?
Anudder
Anudder who?
Anudder mosquito

Knock Knock
Who's there?
Wa
Wa who?
What are you so excited about?

Knock Knock
Who's there?
Gorilla
Gorilla who?
Gorilla me a cheese sandwich

Knock Knock
Who's there?
Barbie
Barbie who?
Barbie-q chicken

Knock Knock
Who's there?
Haven
Haven who?
Haven you hear enough of these jokes?

Knock Knock
Who's there?
Beehive
Beehive who?
Beehive yourself or you're in trouble

Knock Knock
Who's there?
Rhino
Rhino who?
Rhino every knock knock joke there is

Knock Knock
Who's there?
Watts
Watts who?
Watts for dinner, I'm starving

Knock Knock
Who's there?
Ferdie
Ferdie who?
Ferdie last time, open the door

Knock Knock
Who's there?
Amy
Amy who?
Amy fraid I've forgotten

Math Jokes

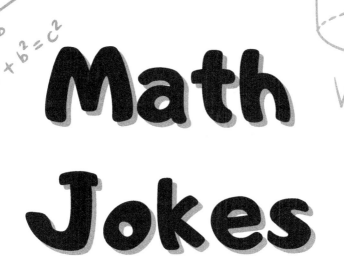

What do you call a number that can't sit still?

- A roamin' numeral

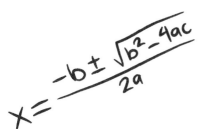

$$x = \frac{-b \pm \sqrt{b^2 - 4ac}}{2a}$$

Why did the math book look so sad?
- Because it had a lot of problems

Where do math teachers go on vacation?
- Times Square

Which tables do you not have to learn?
- Dinner tables

What is the math teacher's favorite dessert?
- Pi

Why did the two fours skip lunch?
- They already eight

What is a butterfly's favorite subject at school?
- Mothematics

Who's in charge of geometry?
- The ruler

1What is a swimmer's favorite type of math?
- Dive-ision

What did the triangle say to the circle?
- You're pointless

How does a mathematician plow fields?
- With a pro-tractor

1.What do you call two dudes who love math?
- Algebros

Why was six afraid of seven?
- Because seven, eight, nine!

What did the calculator say to the student?
- You can always count on me

Do you know what's odd?
- Every other number

What did the bee say when he solved the math problem?
- Hive got it!

Which snakes are good at math?
- Adders

Who invented the round table?
- Sir Cumference

What did the spelling book say to the math book?
- I know I can count on you

What is a math teacher's favorite season?
- Sum-mer

I had an argument with a 90-degree angle.
Turns out it was right

What kind of meals do math teachers eat?
- Square meals

What did the 0 say to the 8?
- **Nice belt**

Why did the triangle make the
basketball team?
- **It always made three-pointers**

What tool is best suited for math?
- **Multi-pliers**

What do mathameticians eat on
Halloween?
- **Pumpkin Pi**

How do you make time fly?
- **Throw the clock out the window**

There are three kinds of people in
this world, those who can count
and those who can't

Why did the girl wear glasses in math
class?
- **It improved di-vision**

What is a math teacher's favorite type of tree?
- Geometry

Who is the king of the pencil case?
- The ruler

What is a witch's favorite shape?
- A hex-agon

Teacher: Why are you doing multiplication on the floor?
Student: You told me not to use tables

Are monsters good at math?
- Not unless you count dracula

How do you make seven an even number?
- Remove the S

What U.S. state has the most math teachers?
- Mathachussets

Parallel lines have so much in common, **it's a shame they'll never meet**

What is a math teacher's favorite snake?
- A pi-thon

What do you call an empty parrot cage?
- A polygon

How are a dollar and the moon similar?
- **They both have four quarters**

What are ten things you can always count on?
- **Your fingers**

Have you heard the latest statistics joke?
- Probably

Have you heard about the mathematical plant?
- It has square roots.

How do you keep warm in a cold room?
- Go to the corner because it's always 90 degrees.

Which king loved fractions?
- Henry the Eighth

What do you get when you cross a math teacher with a clock?
- Mathema-ticks

What is a bird's favorite type of math?
- Owl-gebra

You should never start a conversation with Pi.
- It'll just go on forever

Why wasn't the geometry teacher at school?
- Because she sprained her angle

Why didn't the quarter roll down the hill with the nickle?
- Because it had more cents

Miscellaneous Jokes

How did the baby tell her mom she had a wet diaper?
- She sent her a pee-mail

What did the fisherman say to the magician?
- Pick a cod, any cod

What's a robot's favorite snack?
- Computer chips

What do you call a hippie's wife?
- Mississippi

Why can't a nose be 12 inches long?
- Because then it would be a foot

What has more letters than the alphabet?
- The post office

What's red and smells like blue paint?
- Red paint

What has 4,000 eyes and 8,000 legs?
- 2,000 dogs

What did Mr. and Mrs. Hamburger name their daughter?
- Patty

Where does the general keep his armies?
- Up his sleevies

How does a farmer mend his overalls?
- With cabbage patches

Why did the A go to the bathroom and come out as an E?
- Because he had a vowel movement

What do you call two dinosaurs that have been in an accident?
- Tyrannosaurus Wrecks

What do camels have that no other animal has?
- Baby camels

What do you call a mischievous egg?
- A practical yolker

What's a foot long and slippery?
- A slipper

What do you call a fly in your butter?
- A butterfly

What's the opposite of irony?
- Wrinkly

What do you call a pig that does karate?
- A pork chop

What's the best name for a man who can't stand?
- Neil

What washes up on really small beaches?
- Micro-waves

Why were they called the dark ages?
- Because there were lots of knights

How do fall leaves get from place to place?
- With autumn-mobiles

What did the cupcake tell its frosting?
- I'd be muffin without you

Which hand is better to write with?
- Neither, it's better to write with a pen

If you had 13 grapes, 4 apples, 2 pineapples, and 11 strawberries, what would you have?
- Fruit salad

Why was the librarian kicked off the plane?
- Because it was over booked

What do you get when you cross a caterpillar and a talking parrot?
- A walkie talkie

Why did Cinderella get kicked off of the soccer team?
- Because she kept running from the ball

Some people eat snails,
they must not like fast food

What do you call a pile of kittens?
- A meowntain

What do you call a flea in France?
- A Paris-ite

What is the fastest country in the world?
- Russia

How do I look?
- With your eyes

I have the world's worst thesaurus.
Not only is it terrible, it's also terrible

I tried buying camouflage the other day
but I couldn't find any

How many lips does a flower have?
- Tu-lips

How does a dog stop a video?
- By hitting the paws button

What is the resemblance between a green apple and a red apple?
- They're both red except for the green one

Why do fish avoid computers?
- So they don't get caught on the internet

What did the balloon say to the safety pin?
- Hey, Buster!

What's another name for a snail?
- Booger wearing a helmet

How does a squirrel watch TV?
- Nut-flix

What do you call a cow that can't produce milk?
- An udder failure

What do you call a bee that can't make up its mind?
- A may-bee

Why was the school festival is canceled?
- Because it was no fair

I woke up this morning and forgot which side the sun rises from.
Then it dawned on me

Why couldn't the mummy answer the phone?
- Because she was all tied up

Why was the sand wet?
- Because the sea weed

What do you call a flying policeman?
- A heli-copper

Music Jokes

What did the drummer call
his twin daughters?
- Anna one, Anna two

Why couldn't the athlete listen to her music?
- Because she broke the record

Where did the music teacher leave his keys?
- In the piano

Why did the tortilla chip start dancing?
- Because they put on the salsa

Why did the girl sit on the ladder to sing?
- She wanted to reach the high notes

What type of music are balloons scared of?
- Pop music

What's big and grey with horns?
- An elephant marching band

What do ghosts dance to?
- Soul music

Why did the kid put his head into the piano?
- He wanted to play by ear

Why don't skeletons play music in church?
- Because they don't have any organs

What makes music on your head?
- A head band

Why was the musician arrested?
- Because she got in treble

What music does a planet listen to?
- Nep-tunes

What is a pirate's favorite instrument?
- The guit-arrr

What is the musical part of a snake?
- The scales

What is an avocado's favorite type of music?
- Guac and roll

What is a vampire's favorite part of the guitar?
- The neck

Why did grandma sit in the rocking chair with roller skates on?
- Because she wanted to rock and roll

How do you make a bandstand?
- You take away the chairs

What do you call a dancing sheep?
- A baaah-lerina

What is the loudest pet you can get?
- A trum-pet

What song do monkeys sing at Christmas?
- Jungle Bells

What do you call a singing reptile?
- A rap-tile

What part of a turkey is musical?
- The drumstick

Where did the steak go dancing?
- At the meat ball

What is a cat's favorite song?
- Three blind mice

Why do bagpipe players walk when they play?
- To get away from the noise

What is a cow's favorite music note?
- Beef flat

What is an Egyptian mummy's favorite type of music?
- Rap

How does a witch play loud music?
- On her broom box

What is a bee's favorite classical music composer?
- Bee-thoven

What bone will a dog never eat?
- A trom-bone

What dance style do cars like most?
- Brake dancing

I keep hearing music coming from the printer.
I think the paper is jamming.

What musical instrument do you find in the bathroom?
- A tuba toothpaste

What rock group never sings?
- Mount Rushmore

Where did the frisbee go to dance?
- To the disc-o

How do you get a tuba from the ocean?
- With a tuba diver

Why don't dogs make good dancers?
- Because they have two left feet

How do you fix a broken instrument?
- With a tuba glue

What do you call a cow that can play
a musical instrument?
- A moo-sician

What is the difference between a
fish and a piano?
- You can't tuna fish

What has forty feet and sings?
- The school choir

What is a golfer's favorite type of music?
- Swing

What is a pig's favorite ballet?
- Swine lake

What is a vampire's favorite dance?
- Fango

What do you call a musical insect?
- Humbug

What is a skeleton's favorite instrument?
- The trombone

What is a cucumber's favorite instrument?
- A pickle-o

How does the sun listen to music?
- On the ray-dio

Object Jokes

Why did the boy close his eyes before opening the refrigerator? - He didn't want to see the salad dressing!

HA HA HA

Why are teddy bears never hungry?
- They are always stuffed

Why did the cell phone get glasses?
- Because she lost all her contacts

How do you fix a broken pizza?
- With tomato paste

Why can't toys made from paper move?
- Because they're stationary

What do monkeys wear when they are cooking
- Ape-rons

What's the most popular video game at the bread bakery?
- Knead for Speed.

Why are eyeshadow, lipstick, and mascara never mad at each other?
- Because they always make up

What kind of balls don't bounce?
- Eyeballs

How did the frozen chicken cross the road?
- In a shopping bag

Is a candle happy or sad when you put it out?
- Neither, it's de-lighted

What did the baby find at the end of the rainbow?
- A potty gold

What's it like being a professional yo-yo player?
- It has its ups and downs

Why is it so difficult to sell a toy zebra?
- You can't find the barcode

What has four legs but can't walk?
- A table

What do worms use to leave messages?
- Compost-it-notes

What do you call a dinosaur that takes care of its teeth?
- A Flossiraptor

What bank never has any money?
- A river bank

Where does a sink go dancing?
- The dish-co

What kind of shoes do mice wear?
- Squeakers

What do you call a sweeper that comes back?
- A broom-erang

What did one sock say to the other while in the dryer?
- I'll see you next time around

What do you call a crazy balloon?
- A balloonatic

Man I love my furniture.
Me and my recliner go way back...

What do you call a toy train that eats toffee?
- **A chew chew train**

Is your refrigerator running?
You better go catch it!

How do you start a cuddly toy race?
- **Ready, teddy go!**

What do you call a piece of gold that is afraid of spiders?
- **A chicken nugget**

When is a door not a door?
- **When it's ajar**

Joke Writing Tip:
PRACTICE PRACTICE PRACTICE

JUST LIKE ANYTHING, TO GET BETTER AT WRITING JOKES YOU NEED TO PRACTICE. PRACTICE WRITING JOKES AND PRACTICE TELLING JOKES. OVER TIME YOU WILL FIGURE OUT WHAT WORKS AND WHAT DOESN'T. WITH PRACTICE, YOU WILL BE ABLE TO FIGURE OUT HOW TO GET THE PUNCHLINE JUUUUUUST RIGHT. THE PUNCHLINE IS THE END OF THE JOKE, AND THE BIT THAT MAKES PEOPLE LAUGH. IF THE PUNCHLINE ISN'T RIGHT, THE JOKE WILL FAIL. YOU ALSO WANT TO MAKE SURE YOU ARE CONFIDENT TELLING YOUR JOKE, IF YOU FORGET PART OF IT OR MESS IT UP, IT'S NOT AS FUNNY. SO PRACTICE TELLING THE JOKE IN THE MIRROR UNTIL YOU HAVE IT MEMORIZED, THAT WAY WHEN YOU TELL OTHER PEOPLE YOU WON'T STUMBLE OVER YOUR WORDS. BUT DON'T WORRY, IF YOU DO MESS UP, THAT'S O.K. TOO, JUST COUNT THAT AS A PRACTICE AND TRY AGAIN!

Puns

Don't interrupt someone working intently on a puzzle. Chances are, you'll hear some crosswords

I'm reading a book about anti-gravity.
It's impossible to put down!

I hate beards,
but they're growing on me!

Need an ark to save two of
every animal?
I Noah guy

Thanks for explaining the word
"many" to me
It means a lot

You really shouldn't be intimidated
by advanced math,
It's easy as pi

To the man who invented zero,
thanks for nothing

I asked a French man if he played
video games.
He said wii

Coffee has a rough time in our household,
It gets mugged every single morning

I can't believe I got fired from the calendar factory,
all I did was take a day off

Waking up this morning was an eye-opening experience

Being a vegetarian is one big missed steak

I stayed up all night to see where the sun went,
then it dawned on me

I lost my mood ring the other day,
I'm not sure how I feel about it

My leaf blower doesn't work,
It just sucks

A book just fell on my head.
I only have myshelf to blame.

I wrote a song about a tortilla.
Actually, it's more of a wrap.

Of course I ate my homework!
The teacher said it's a piece of cake.

Pigs are no fun to hang around.
They're just a boar.

Geology rocks,
but geography is where it's at

Long fairy tales tend to
dragon

I knew a guy who collected
candy canes,
they were all in mint condition

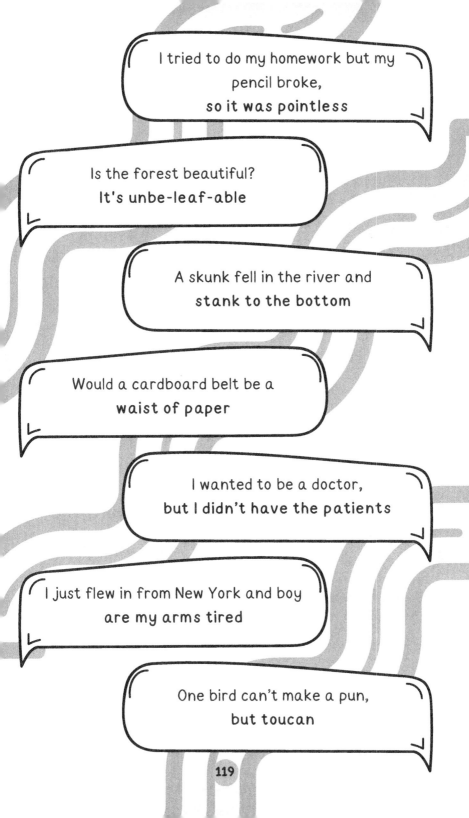

I tried to do my homework but my pencil broke,
so it was pointless

Is the forest beautiful?
It's unbe-leaf-able

A skunk fell in the river and
stank to the bottom

Would a cardboard belt be a
waist of paper

I wanted to be a doctor,
but I didn't have the patients

I just flew in from New York and boy
are my arms tired

One bird can't make a pun,
but toucan

I just found out I'm colorblind.
The diagnosis came completely out
of the purple

I ate an alarm clock yesterday.
It was very time-consuming

When life gives you melons
you might be a little confused

The problem with thieves is that they
always take things literally

People say I'm indecisive
but I'm not so sure

I tried to have my doctor treat my
case of invisibility,
but he said he couldn't see me

If you take care of a chicken
are you a chicken tender?

School Jokes

Why did the egg get thrown out of class?
- Because he kept telling yolks

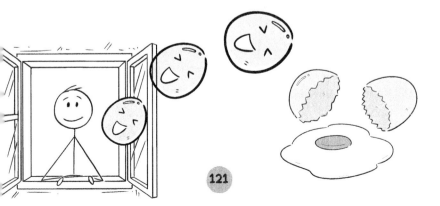

Why did the jellybean go to school?
- To become a smartie

How do bees get to school?
- The school buzz

Why was the broom late for school?
- He over swept

What do you do if a cat swallows
your pencil?
- Use a pen

Why did the cyclops close his school?
- Because he only had one pupil

Why did the dog do so well in school?
- Because he was the teacher's pet

What is a witch's favorite subject
in school?
- Spelling

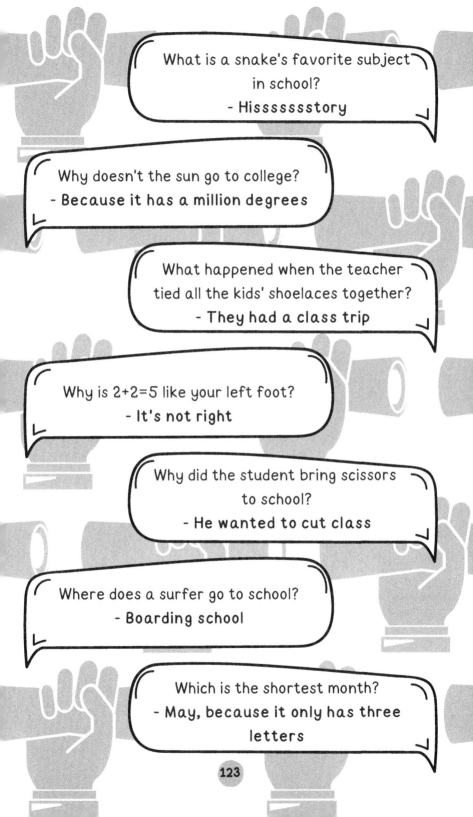

What is a snake's favorite subject in school?
- Hisssssssstory

Why doesn't the sun go to college?
- Because it has a million degrees

What happened when the teacher tied all the kids' shoelaces together?
- They had a class trip

Why is 2+2=5 like your left foot?
- It's not right

Why did the student bring scissors to school?
- He wanted to cut class

Where does a surfer go to school?
- Boarding school

Which is the shortest month?
- May, because it only has three letters

Why did the teacher go to the beach?
- **To test the water**

What is the difference between a train and a teacher?
- **One says spit your gum out, the other says "choo, choo"**

What's the worst thing that can happen to a geography teacher?
- **Getting lost**

What flies around school at night?
- **The alpha-bat**

Why do we measure snakes in inches?
- **Because they do not have feet**

What do you call a square that's been in an accident?
- **A wreck-tangle**

What is a blackboards favorite drink?
- **Hot chalk-olate**

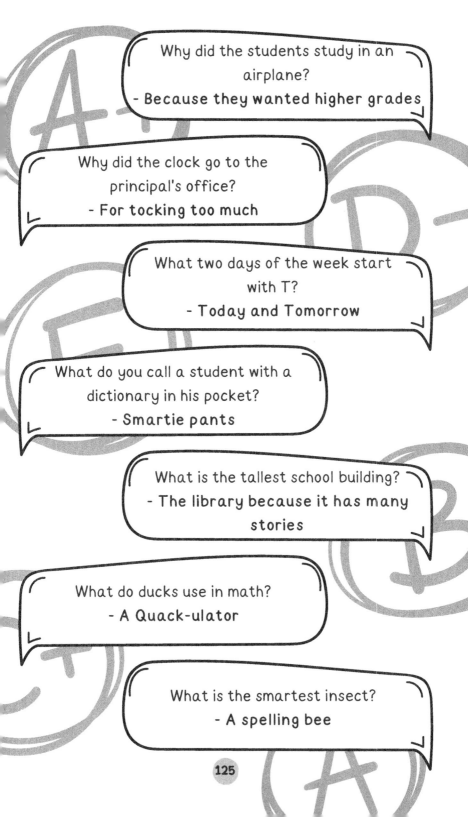

Why did the students study in an airplane?
- Because they wanted higher grades

Why did the clock go to the principal's office?
- For tocking too much

What two days of the week start with T?
- Today and Tomorrow

What do you call a student with a dictionary in his pocket?
- Smartie pants

What is the tallest school building?
- The library because it has many stories

What do ducks use in math?
- A Quack-ulator

What is the smartest insect?
- A spelling bee

What does a thesaurus eat for breakfast?
- A synonym roll

Why did the echo get detentions?
- It kept answering back

How many letters are in the alphabet?
- 11, T-H-E-A-L-P-H-A-B-E-T

What did the ghost teacher say to her class?
- Watch the board and I'll go through it again

Why did the snake get detention?
- Because he was hisspering in class

Did you hear about the cross-eyed teacher?
- He couldn't control his pupils

What becomes smaller when you turn it upside down?
- The number 9

Where is the best place to grow flowers in school?
- In Kindergarden

Which letter of the alphabet has the most water?
- The C

What do you do if a teacher rolls her eyes at you?
- Pick them up and roll them back

Why did the teacher wear sunglasses to school?
- Because her students were too bright

What letter is hidden in a mug?
- T

Teacher: Why did you eat your homework?
Student: Because I don't have a dog

Why did the broom get poor grades?
- Because he was always sweeping in class

Why was school easier for cave people?
- Because there was no history

What time would it be if Godzilla came to school?
- Time to run

What did the buffalo say at school drop off?
- Bison

Why did the kid bring a ladder to school?
- Because she wanted to go to high school

What dinosaur has the best vocabulary?
- Thesaurus

What does a book do in the winter?
- Put on a jacket

Why do magicians do so well in school?
- They can handle trick questions

Science Jokes

What is the opposite of a
cold front?

- A warm back

Why did the cloud date the fog?
- He was so down to earth

Why are chemists so good at solving problems?
- They are always working with solutions

Why did the cow go to space?
- To visit the milky way

What did one tectonic plate say when he bumped into another?
- Sorry! My fault

Wanna hear a mountain joke?
- Nah, you won't get over it

What do you call a tick on the moon?
- A lunar-tick

How do spacemen kill time?
- They play astronauts and crosses

What did the science book say to the math book?
- You've got problems

What is a tornado's favorite game to play?
- Twister

Why did the sun go to school?
- To get brighter

How do hurricanes see?
- With one eye

What do clouds wear?
- Thunderwear

What was the first animal to go into space?
- The cow that jumped over the moon

Where did the scientist eat his lunch?
- At the periodic table

131

What did the tornado say to the washing machine?
- Want to go for a spin

What's the name of the first electricity detective?
- Sherlock Ohms

How much room do fungi need to grow?
- As mushroom as possible

What bow can't be tied?
- A rainbow

How do scientists freshen their breath?
- With experi-mints

What did the Atlantic Ocean say to the Pacific Ocean?
- Nothing, Oceans don't talk, they wave!

What is a spaceman's favorite chocolate?
- A mars bar

How do you know the moon is going broke?
- **It's down to its last quarter**

How do you cut the sea in half?
- **With a see saw**

Why did the leaf go to the doctor?
- **It was feeling green**

I try to tell chemistry jokes but...
there is no reaction

What can run, but cannot walk?
- **Water**

Why did the scientist take out his doorbell?
- **He wanted to win the no-bell prize**

What kind of hair do oceans have?
- **Wavy**

How do you know that Saturn is married?
- Because it has a big ring

Why is wind power popular?
- Because it has a lot of fans

Where do astronauts pay for parking?
- Parking meteors

What happens when it rains cats and dogs?
- You might step in a poodle

Why is electricity an ideal citizen?
- Because it conducts itself well

Why did the germ cross the microscope?
- To get to the other slide

What did the cloud say to the lightning bolt?
- You're shocking

Why don't aliens eat clowns?
- Because they taste funny

I know another science joke...
- It's on the tip of my tungsten

What's the difference between weather and climate?
- You can't weather a tree but you can climate

What is a king's favorite weather?
- Hail

What did the volcano say to his wife?
- I lava you

What music do planets dance to?
- Nep-tunes

How did Benjamin Franklin feel after discovering electricity?
- Shocked

What runs faster, cold or hot?
- Hot, because you can catch a cold

What did one raindrop say to the other raindrop?
- My plop is bigger than your plop

How do you know when the moon has had enough to eat?
- When it's full

How do you throw a party in space?
- You plan-et

What is a pirate's favorite element?
- Arrrrgon

Why shouldn't you fight a cloud?
- He'll storm out on you

What falls but never hits the ground?
- The temperature

Spooky Jokes

Who are the werewolf's cousins?
- The what-wolf and the when-wolf

Why did the witches' team lose the baseball game?
- Because their bats flew away

Where do ghosts buy their food?
- At the Ghostery store

What kind of bees eat brains?
- Zombees

How does a ghost sneeze?
- Ahh...ahh...ahh...BOO!

How do ghosts like their eggs?
- Terri-fried

What time is it when the clock strikes 13?
- Time to get a new clock

Where do vampires keep their money?
- The blood bank

What is a ghosts favorite food?
- Boo-berries

Why did the ghost blow its nose?
- Because it was full of booo-gers

What did the skeleton order for dinner?
- Spare ribs

Do zombies eat brains with their fingers?
- Nope, they eat everything separately

What do skeletons fly around in?
- A skelecopter

What position does a ghost play
in hockey?
- Ghoulie

What happens when a ghost gets lost
in the fog?
- He is mist

What is a zombies favorite toy?
- His deady bear

What's the problem with twin witches?
- You can never tell which
witch is which

What sound do witches make when
they eat cereal?
- Snap, cackle and pop

Why did the skeleton go to jail?
- He was bad to the bone

What do witches race on?
- Vroomsticks

Why didn't the skeleton dance?
- Because he had no body to dance
with

What do you call a witch with
chicken pox?
- An itchy witchy

Where do baby ghosts go during the day?
- Day scare

What do you get if you cross Bambi with a ghost?
- Bamboo

How do zombies greet new people?
- Pleased to eat you

What's a skeleton's favorite fruit?
- Bone-anas

Where do zombies go on vacation?
- The dead seas

What kind of tests do vampires take at school?
- Blood tests

Why did the zombie skip school?
- He felt rotten

141

Why are vampires like false teeth?
- They come out at night

What do witches put on their bagels?
- Scream cheese

What does it take to become a zombie?
- Dead-ication

What is the national holiday for vampires?
- Fangs-giving

When is it bad luck to be followed by a black cat?
- When you are a mouse

What is a vampire's favorite fruit?
- A neck-tarine

Who won the skeleton beauty contest?
- No body

142

What is a ghosts favorite meal?
- Spook-ghetti

What room does a ghost not need?
- A living room

What do zombies read every morning?
- Their horror-scope

What monster plays tricks on Halloween?
- Prank-enstein

What do you call two witches sharing an apartment?
- Broommates

What does an Australian witch fly on?
- A Broom-erang

What did one ghost say to the other ghost?
- Do you believe in people?

What does a skeleton say before he eats?
- Bone appetite

When does a ghost have breakfast?
- In the moaning

How do you make a milk shake?
- Give it a good scare

What is black and white a dead all over?
- A zombie penguin

What did one ghost say to the other ghost?
- Get a life

Who is the skeleton king of rock and roll?
- Pelvis

What do ghosts use to wash their hair?
- Sham-boo

Sport Jokes

Why does a pitcher raise one leg when he throws the ball?
- Because if he raised them both he'd fall down

What did the coach say to the broken vending machine?
- I want my quarter back

Why did the basketball player bring his suitcase to the game?
- Because he traveled a lot

What is the hardest part of skydiving?
- The ground

What did the baseball glove say to the ball?
- Catch you later

Why can't you play soccer in the jungle?
- There are too many cheetahs

When is a baby good at basketball?
- When it's dribbling

What did the skeleton drive to the hockey game?
- The zam-bony

Why didn't the fish play basketball?
- Because he was afraid of the net

When is a baseball player like a spider?
- When he catches a fly

Why are bowling alleys so quiet?
- So you can hear a pin drop

What do you give a hockey player
when he demands to be paid?
- A check

What goes all the way around the
baseball field but never moves?
- The fence

Why do basketball players love donuts?
- Because they can dunk them

What do scuba divers wear to bed?
- A snore-kel

Why did the basketball player go to jail?
- Because he shot the ball

What can you serve but never eat?
- A tennis ball

Why is tennis such a loud sport?
- The players raise a racquet

How is a baseball team similar to pancakes?
- They both need a good batter

What sport are eggs best at?
- Running

What is an insect's favorite sport?
- Cricket

Why are hockey rinks always rounded?
- Because if they were 90 degrees, then the ice would melt

What do vampires eat at halftime?
- Blood oranges

Why did the chicken get sent off the sporting field?
- Fowl play

Why didn't the dog want to play football?
- It was a boxer

What time do tennis players go to bed?
- Tennish

Why did the ballerina quit?
- Because it was tu-tu hard

What is a sheep's favorite game?
- Baaa-dminton

What do a hockey player and a magician have in common?
- They both do hat tricks

Which baseball player can hold water the best?
- The pitcher

What sport do hairdressers love most?
- Curling

Why are basketball courts always wet?
- Because the players always dribble

What does the sun skate on?
- Solarblades

What's a ball you don't throw, shoot, eat, spit, bounce or catch?
- An eyeball

How do bunnies stay fit?
- Hare-robics

What is a bee's favorite sport?
- Rug-bee

What is a golfer's favorite letter?
- Tee

What do you call a girl standing in the middle of a tennis court?
- Annette

What animal is best at hitting a baseball?
- A bat

What sport do wasps play?
- Sting pong

What is a frog's favorite game?
- Leapfrog

What kind of race is never run?
- A swimming race

What is harder to catch the faster you run?
- Your breath

What do you get when a dinosaur scores a touchdown?
- A dino-score

What do you call a monkey who wins the sporting match?
- The Chimp-ion

What are the rules for zebra baseball?
- Three stripes and you're out

When is a baseball player like a criminal?
- When he steals a base

What is a math teacher's favorite sport?
- Figure skating

How do you start a firefly race?
- Ready, set, glow

What sporting event do pigs hold every four years?
- The Olympigs

Technology Jokes

Why did the computer cross the road?

- To get a byte to eat

How do trees get on the internet?
- They log in

What did the spider do on the computer?
- Made a website

What do robots drink from?
- A robottle

What do you get when you cross a computer with a crocodile?
- A mega biter

Where do computers keep their money?
- In a data bank

Why did the computer keep sneezing?
- It had a virus

How do clams call their friends?
- On their shell phones

What do you call the woman who married the internet?
- The wife-i

What do tooth fairies have on their phones?
- Bluetooth

What did the man say to his dead robot?
- Rust in peace

What did the turkey say to the computer?
- Google google google

Why did the computer go to the eye doctor?
- To improve its web-sight

Where do robots sit?
- On their robottoms

Why was the computer cold?
- It left windows open

How many cops does it take to screw in a lightbulb?
- None, it turns itself in

Why was the computer late?
- It had a hard drive

Why is the computer so smart?
- It listens to its motherboard

How did the mobile phone propose to his girlfriend?
- He gave her a ring

What do robots wear in winter?
- Roboots

Where do computers go dancing?
- The disc-o

Why are dogs like phones?
- Because they have collar IDs

Why did the computer go to the dentist?
- It had a blue tooth

Why did the wifi marry the computer?
- They had a connection

Why did the computer squeak?
- Because someone stepped on its mouse

What do you get when you cross a computer and a lifeguard?
- A screensaver

Where does a robot go on holiday?
- Wireland

What are computers' favorite snacks?
- Computer chips

How does a computer eat?
- With mega-bytes

Joke Writing Tip:

LAUGH AT YOURSELF

HAVE YOU EVER NOTICED THAT SOME OF THE FUNNIEST JOKES PEOPLE MAKE ARE JOKES ABOUT THEMSELVES? LEARNING TO LAUGH AT YOURSELF CAN BE REALLY TOUGH, ESPECIALLY IF YOU MAKE A JOKE ABOUT YOURSELF AND EVERYONE LAUGHS, THEN YOU FEEL LIKE PEOPLE ARE LAUGHING AT YOU. THE DIFFERENCE IS THAT WHEN YOU LAUGH AT YOURSELF, PEOPLE AREN'T LAUGHING AT YOU, THEY ARE LAUGHING WITH YOU. WE CAN ALSO MAKE REALLY FUNNY JOKES ABOUT OURSELVES THAT WE CAN'T MAKE ABOUT OTHER PEOPLE. FOR EXAMPLE, IF I TELL A JOKE ABOUT SOMETHING EMBARRASSING THAT I DID, THAT'S TOTALLY FINE, BUT IF I TELL A JOKE ABOUT THE SAME EMBARRASSING THING THAT MY FRIEND DID, THAT'S MEAN. DO YOU SEE THE DIFFERENCE? BEING ABLE TO LAUGH AT YOURSELF MEANS YOU HAVE MORE CONTENT TO MAKE JOKES FROM, AND WHO DOESN'T WANT MORE JOKES?!

Toilet Jokes

When is the best time to go to the toilet?
- Poo-thirty

Why did the toilet roll down the hill?
- To get to the bottom

Why did the superhero flush the toilet?
- Because it was his doody

Did you hear about the film 'Constipated'?
- It never came out

Where is the best place to go pee?
- IP address

Why did one kid bring toilet paper to the party?
- He was a party pooper

What's invisible and smells like worms?
- A bird fart

There are two reasons you shouldn't drink from the toilet
- Number one and number two!

Why did three witches call in a plumber?
- Hubble, bubble, toilet trouble

What did the poo say to the fart?
- You blow me away

Why did the baker's hands stink?
- He kneaded a poo

What do you call a peeing magician?
- A wizard

What's the German word for constipation?
- Farfrompoopen

What did one toilet say to the other?
- You look a little flushed

What do you call superman with diarrhea?
- Pooperman

The toilet at my local police station has been stolen,
Cops have nothing to go on

Who are the most dangerous farters in the world?
- Ninjas. They're silent but deadly

Why didn't the toilet paper make it across the road?
- It got stuck in the crack

What sort of dog can you find in a bathroom?
- A poodle

Why do people take naps on the toiler?
- Because it's a restroom

What do you call a fairy that uses the toilet?
- Stinker Bell

Want to join the wee-wee club?
- Urine!

Why did the police officer sit on the toiler?
- To do his duty

What do octopuses do after using the toilet?
- They wash their hands, hands, hands hands, hands, hands, hands, hands

What's the best snack for watching a movie?
- Poop corn

Poop jokes aren't my favorite jokes, but they're a solid number two

What did the puma say to his friend who was making poop jokes?
"Stop making me laugh or I'll puma pants"

Today I learned that diarrhea is hereditary,
it runs in your jeans

What do you call a magical poop?
- Poodini

Joke Writing Tip:

NOTEBOOK

THIS SEEMS LIKE SUCH A SIMPLE TIP, BUT IT WILL REALLY MAKE A DIFFERENCE TO YOUR JOKE WRITING IF YOU TRY IT. GET A DEDICATED 'JOKE NOTEBOOK' AND CARRY IT WITH YOU. THAT WAY, EVERY TIME YOU HAVE AN IDEA, YOU CAN QUICKLY JOT IT DOWN IN YOUR NOTEBOOK BEFORE YOU FORGET. YOU CAN (AND SHOULD) ALSO USE THE NOTEBOOK TO WRITE DOWN ANYTHING FUNNY THAT HAPPENS DURING THE DAY. THIS WILL HELP YOU COME UP WITH JOKE IDEAS WHEN YOU NEED THEM. WRITE DOWN JOKES YOU HEARD THAT WERE FUNNY, THINGS THAT MADE YOU LAUGH, THINGS THAT MADE OTHER PEOPLE LAUGH, ANYTHING AND EVERYTHING FUNNY SHOULD GO IN THAT BOOK. THEN, WHEN YOU FEEL INSPIRED, SIT DOWN WITH YOUR BOOK AND GO THROUGH IT AND TURN YOUR NOTES INTO JOKES!

Transport Jokes

What happened to the
wooden car?
- It wooden go

How often do airplanes crash?
- Just once

What do you call a train with a cold?
- Achoo Achoo train

How do you get to tooth island?
- The tooth ferry

What do you need to be able to
drive in the outback?
- You need to show your koala-fications

What do you call a sleeping bull?
- A bull dozer

Why can't cars play football?
- Because they only have one boot

What do you call a helicopter with
a cold?
- A heli-coughter

How can you tell if a train just went by?
- You can see its tracks

Why did the taxi driver lose his job?
- He kept driving his customers away

What do you call a snail on a ship?
- A snailor

What is the most tired part of your car?
- The exhaust pipe

Why did the bus stop?
- Because it saw a zebra crossing

What is the worst vegetable to serve on a boat?
- Leeks

Why did the airplane get sent to his room?
- Bad altitude

How did the train get so good at its job?
- Training

What's as big as a steam train but weighs nothing?
- Its shadow

Why did the robot sleep under a car?
- He wanted to wake up oily

How do you get four dragons into a car?
- Two in the front, two in the back

What do you call a very fast llama?
- A llamaghini

How do fleas travel from place to place?
- By itch-hiking

Did you hear about the ice cream truck that crashed?
- The driver blamed it on the rocky road

How did the lobster get to the ocean?
- By Shell-icopter

What part of the car is the laziest?
- The wheels, because they are always tired

How do trains hear?
- Through the engine-ears

Where is the best place to sit on a submarine?
- Inside

Two goldfish are in a tank. One says to the other
"do you know how to drive this thing?"

What is worse than raining cats and dogs?
- Hailing taxis

What brand of motorcycle laughs the most?
- Yamahahaha

Joke Writing Tip:

PUT YOURSELF IN A FUNNY MOOD

WHETHER YOU ARE WRITING JOKES OR TELLING JOKES, YOU WANT TO MAKE SURE YOU ARE FEELING GREAT BEFORE YOU START. IMAGINE TRYING TO MAKE PEOPLE LAUGH WHEN YOU ARE FEELING TIRED OR CRANKY. SO BEFORE YOU START JOKING, PREPARE YOURSELF BY PUTTING YOURSELF IN A FUNNY MOOD. THERE ARE LOTS OF WAYS TO DO THIS. SOME GOOD THINGS TO TRY ARE READING YOUR FAVORITE JOKES, LISTENING TO A FUNNY COMEDIAN, MAKING FUNNY FACES OR NOISES, THINKING OF SOMETHING FUNNY THAT HAPPENED RECENTLY. OR, THIS IS MY PERSONAL FAVORITE - JUST START LAUGHING! FAKE A LAUGH FOR AS LONG AS POSSIBLE AND I PROMISE YOU THAT PRETTY SOON YOU WILL START LAUGHING AND YOU WON'T BE ABLE TO STOP!

Chicken Jokes

Why did the chicken cross the road?

- Just beak-cause he could

Why did the dinosaur cross the road?
- Because the chicken wasn't invented yet

Why did the chicken run across the road?
- To get to the other side faster

Why did the chicken cross the road?
- To bock traffic

Why did the chicken cross the playground?
- To get to the other slide

Why did the turkey cross the road?
- To prove he wasn't chicken

Why did the sheep cross the road?
- To get to the baa-baa shop for a haircut

Why did the cow cross the road?
- To get to the udder side

Why did the rooster cross the road?
- He had something to cock-a-doodle dooo

Why did the dog cross the road twice?
- He was playing fetch with a boomerang

Why did the fish cross the ocean?
- To get to the other tide

How did the egg cross the road?
- It scrambled across

Why didn't the chicken cross the road?
- Because there was a fried chicken shop on the other side

Why did the duck cross the road?
- Because it thought it was a chicken

Why did the monkey cross the road?
- Because the chicken retired

Why did the man with no hands cross the road?
- To get to the second-hand shop

Why did the robot cross the road?
- Because the chicken was out of order

Why did the nose cross the road?
- Because he was tired of getting picked on

Why did the dog cross the road?
- Because he was chasing the chicken

Why did the zebra cross the road?
- Because it was a zebra crossing

How did the fish cross the road?
- In flip flops

Why couldn't the toilet paper cross the road?
- It got stuck in a crack

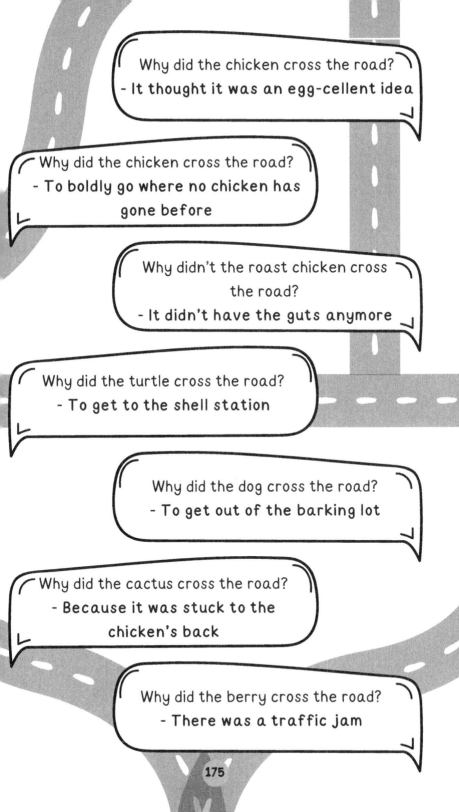

Why did the chicken cross the road?
- It thought it was an egg-cellent idea

Why did the chicken cross the road?
- To boldly go where no chicken has gone before

Why didn't the roast chicken cross the road?
- It didn't have the guts anymore

Why did the turtle cross the road?
- To get to the shell station

Why did the dog cross the road?
- To get out of the barking lot

Why did the cactus cross the road?
- Because it was stuck to the chicken's back

Why did the berry cross the road?
- There was a traffic jam

Why did the gum cross the road?
- It was stuck to the chicken's foot

Why did the horse cross the road?
- He wanted to see his neigh-bor

What happened when the elephant crossed the road?
- It stepped on the chicken

Why did the potato cross the road?
- So it wouldn't get mashed

Why didn't the flamingo cross the road?
- It isn't a chicken

Why did the Easter Bunny cross the road?
- The chicken had his eggs

Why did the pillow cross the road?
- It was picking up the chicken's feathers

Why did the clown cross the road?
- To get his rubber chicken

Why did the raccoon cross the road?
- Because it saw garbage on the other side

Why did the chicken cross the road?
- To get to the other side

The

End

Printed in Great Britain
by Amazon